CLOSE
to the Broken

A 30 DAY HEALING CHALLENGE

TIANA MCKAN

Copyright © 2021 by Tiana McKan

All rights reserved. No part of this book may be reproduced, scanned, or distributed in any printed or electronic form without permission.

This book is dedicated to the black sheep. The person that feels like they do not belong. The person that feels like they are furthest from God. This is for you. This is for us. Remember that God is closest to the broken, and He uses broken people to make masterpieces.

Introduction

Danger of A Broken Heart

You're hurting and you're broken. Life is cold and you feel alone. Life is wearing you down, but you put on a mask and pretend that everything is okay and that you are fine. This was me. The pain of neglect, abuse and betrayal lingered at the core of my being. At one point it left me high and dry; and I did not know who I was. My heart was broken, but to avoid feeling my emotions I self-medicated with numbing gel. It's that door you keep closed and locked away hoping to never open again, but when it does accidentally swing open you must quickly pick up the pieces, slam the door shut and find your mask so you can proceed like everything is okay. Because after all, you are fine, and life is great! You are blessed and highly favored, right? Wrong.

It's okay to not be okay. It's okay to be hurt, angry and sad. When you wear the "everything is fine" mask, you hurt yourself more than you hurt anyone else; and block yourself from getting help. You are also not being honest with yourself which hinders you from being able to heal from the pain that you are numbing yourself from. But no one will understand your struggles, right? The devil has a funny way of making you feel like you are alone and that God wants nothing to do with a mess like you. The devil's job is to make you feel separated from God. If the devil can isolate you from God, then he can tamper with your thoughts and play on your emotions. A broken heart is the devil's playground. If he sees one spot he can use against you, trust me he will. The devil's job is to kill, steal and destroy.

Proverbs 4:23 says, *"Above all else, guard your heart, for everything you do flows from it."* This scripture is about the condition of the heart. What state is your heart in? Really reflect on this. If your heart is broken or sick, broken and sick actions will flow out of it. This means that you will stay in relationships that God has told you to let go of; you will avoid forming social relationships or you will become overly clingy to others; you will continue to self-medicate by using drugs; and/or you will engage in promiscuity. This is because you are looking to fill the cracks and missing pieces of your broken heart. These temporary earthly solutions will help you only for a moment, but when you are all alone and your access to these things is no longer available, then what will you do?

I have been saved for years, and if you ask me what I think about God, I'd tell you He is loving and only wants the best for us. I have been in relationships I knew were toxic for me, but I stayed because I was comfortable in the chaos, and it felt safe to me. My broken heart hindered me from trusting God. Instead, I chose to continue harming myself by trying to "mend" my heart with new toxic relationships and deliberately choosing to be disobedient to God. My sick and broken heart from my past caused me to struggle to trust God and His Word. At times I felt so condemned. I felt like I could not pray to God or even look in His direction because I was such a mess. I felt ashamed. I had never felt so distant from God, but whose voice was I listening to?

God does not condemn. He does not want us to be unhappy. He does not want us to feel alone. He loves us and when we are weak, He is strong, and will carry us through our mess. Isaiah 40:29 states, *"He gives strength to the weary and increases the power of the weak."* God is close to the brokenhearted. He sent His son, Jesus, to die on the cross for broken people like me and you. He does not expect us to be perfect. He wants a relationship with us, and when you get to know Him you will begin to understand the desires of His heart for you. Trust Him as you go through this healing journey. I pray that this book is a blessing to you and that it will help you to heal through your hurt. God has taught me each of the lessons shared as I continue to travel through my own healing journey. Blessings to you. Remember that God is close, and His love is unconditional.

Day 1
Hearing from God

"And he said, "Go out and stand on the mount before the Lord." And behold, the Lord passed by, and a great and strong wind tore the mountains and broke in pieces the rocks before the Lord, but the Lord was not in the wind. And after the wind an earthquake, but the Lord was not in the earthquake. And after the earthquake a fire, but the Lord was not in the fire. And after the fire the sound of a low whisper. And when Elijah heard it, he wrapped his face in his cloak and went out and stood at the entrance of the cave. And behold, there came a voice to him and said, "What are you doing here, Elijah?""

-1 Kings19:11-13

Before we dig into forgiveness, I want you to know that this book is meant to guide you through your journey of forgiveness and healing. This means that you have to put forth the effort to apply what you read to your life. The word healing is a verb which means that ACTION has to occur in order for change to come. As you read this book, you have to keep an open mind. You also have to really apply what is being said to your life and allow it to seep into your thoughts and spirit.

The most important assignment in this book is understanding your language with God. I want you to ponder on how God speaks to you. Do you experience visions, vivid dreams, profound thoughts, strong feelings, things in nature, His word, smells? There are so many ways God speaks, but what is your personal language with Him? God is always speaking and showing us things, but we don't always listen. We expect Him to speak to us in a certain way, but God is not limited. People expect major things to happen when God speaks, but I have personally learned it is the subtle things that God typically uses to speak. If you are not aware, you will miss it. Knowing how God communicates with you is essential because God is going to meet you where you are during this healing journey, but you have to let Him guide you, so do not limit Him. Don't put God in a box because you will miss Him. Pay attention to your feelings throughout this process. If something occurs that reminds you of your past hurt, do not be afraid. Often times we blame the devil, but be open and prayerful because it may be God showing you where it still hurts in order to properly heal you. Prayer is key in this journey. Remember, prayer is just a casual conversation with God.

Challenge

Make a list of the different ways you hear from God.

Prayer

Heavenly Father, I pray that you would open my eyes, ears and heart so that I can see the personal language you have with me. Make yourself present as I go through this journey. Help me to discern your voice from my own. In Jesus name I pray, Amen.

Day 2
Understanding Who God Is

"Love is patient and kind; love does not envy or boast; it is not arrogant or rude. It does not insist on its own way; it is not irritable or resentful; it does not rejoice at wrongdoing, but rejoices with the truth. Love bears all things, believes all things, hopes all things, endures all things. Love never ends."

-2 Corinthians 13:4-8

This journey is primarily between you and God. In order to really build your relationship with God you have to know who He is. It is so easy to project human characteristics onto God. For example, feeling like you cannot depend on Him because you have been surrounded with unreliable people. I have also seen people project characteristics of their mother or father onto God. For example, my father abandoned me, so why would God love someone like me? He will probably abandon me too. My personal example is due to my struggle with perfectionism. I allowed the hardships I put on myself to reflect in my relationship with God. For example, when I felt like I messed up or maybe did not do things 100 percent, I just knew God was up there with His checklist like, "Nope, that's an x. I asked her one simple thing why can't she get it right." Honestly that was my viewpoint of myself. I projected my own thoughts onto God. God is not like any human that we know. His love is unconditional. His ways are not our ways, and His thoughts are not like ours. He is a safe place. We can approach Him and talk without judgement. Not only this, but He is also a gentleman. He does not force Himself on you, but waits until you are ready to receive Him. We will never fully understand His goodness because it is not natural, but in order to build a stronger relationship with Him, you have to make sure you are discarding any human characteristics you are putting on Him because He is not human, He is GOD! He is the true definition of love. We love because He first loved us (1 John 4:19).

Challenge

Identify the human characteristics you place on God, then find scriptures that will help you discover who He is.

Prayer

Dear God, thank you for your unconditional love for me. Forgive me for comparing you to people that have hurt me. Reveal to me the false perceptions of you that I carry, so that I can let it go and grow closer to you. Help me to see you for the amazing Father that you are. In Jesus name, Amen.

Day 3

Dangers of Unforgiveness

"Do not bear a grudge against others, but settle your differences with them, so that you will not commit a sin because of them. Do not take revenge on others or continue to hate them, but love your neighbors as you love yourself. I am the Lord." -Leviticus 19:17-18

Have you ever wondered why you struggle to trust people like strangers or even people close to you? Or why you are so easily offended? You always have your guard up and struggle to put your hair down. You struggle to maintain healthy relationships, both casual and romantic. Unforgiveness is a silent thief. The residue from unforgiveness can seep into other areas of your life and destroy it. Unforgiveness is a crack in your foundation that gives the devil the opportunity to sneak in and destroy whatever he can. Operating in unforgiveness is like wearing broken glasses. It divides your vision, causing you to struggle to see the world from the clear perspective God wants you to see it from because of the offenses and pain you hold on to. You see life from hurt places, which distorts your vision from what is actually happening.

For example, you got your heart broken by someone you really cared about. Now you have hardened your heart and built walls to keep others from hurting you again. Anytime someone tries to come close to you, you cut them off because you are determined to not get hurt like you did in the relationship that broke your heart six years ago. How are you going to be the willing vessel God called you to be when you are holding on to pain and unforgiveness; and can no longer see the bigger picture, but only a fraction of the picture due to the cracks in your glasses? You have a distorted view and you may not even realize it because it has been that way for years. I want you to understand the dangers of living this way. Viewing the world with a cracked lens causes division. Unforgiveness divides our relationships with others, divides our health (emotional and/or physical), and above all it divides our relationship with God. It divides our relationship with God because it takes away our prayer life and distorts the way we see Him, which can lead us to put up walls against God without even realizing it. But you wonder why you struggle to hear God when you pray? It may be due to the dividers you placed between you and God. God is not going to give you what you pray for until you become the person that is able to receive it. Yes, unforgiveness may seem like the easiest route in the beginning, but over time it takes more from you than you are willing to give. It takes your peace of mind, health and support, and hardens your heart, distances you from God, delays your blessings, and so much more. Ask yourself, how much am I going to let unforgiveness take from me before I decide to let it go?

Challenge

Make a list of what unforgiveness has cost you, and what it will cost you if you continue to dwell in it.

Prayer

Heavenly Father, choosing to forgive is not easy, but I am trusting you to help me through this journey. Please show me the areas that unforgiveness has caused division in my life. Help me to mend the division that was created and forgive me for holding on to ill emotions. Repair my broken lens so I can see life the way you intended with a clear view. In Jesus name, Amen.

Day 4

What Is Forgiveness

"The righteous shall move onward and forward; those with pure hearts shall become stronger and stronger." -Job 17:9

When someone is giving you something how is your hand postured? Do you accept it with your hands open wide or tightly closed? The answer seems simple, right? Your hand has to be open wide in order to receive something. So how do you expect God to give you the desires of your heart when you hold on to your past offenses so tightly? Why do you refuse to let go of the things that have hurt you? Forgiveness is the ability to LET GO. Let go of the pain, let go of the hurt, let go of the anger, let go of the self-doubt, let go of the ill emotions. LET IT GO. Have you ever held on to something so long your fingers began to cramp? Unforgiveness is like that cramp you experience. It brings its own pain along with the current pain you feel from a past event. The truth is anything can be forgiven, it's just up to you whether or not you want to do it.

Forgiveness can be challenging and look different depending on the situation. Some offenses may have you in your "feelings" so much so that you do not want to forgive, but you have to understand that a broken heart is deceptive. Your "feelings" will lead to more hurt. Think about it. The longer you hold your hand tightly closed, the more intense the pain becomes overtime. God knows the danger of unforgiveness, which is why He requires us to forgive so that we can live the life He designed for us. When you choose to forgive, you are trusting that God will bless the situation and turn it around for your good. When you decide to let go you will feel relieved; and will be able to live life with true peace. Forgiveness is a gift for you. When you choose to forgive, you are choosing to be free. It legitimately feels like weights lifted off of you when you choose to forgive.

The beautiful thing about believing in God is when you let go and forgive, you are giving it to a God who will take care of it for you. God is amazing. He will fight your battles for you, all you have to do is let go. When we hold on to things that are not meant for us, this is when we experience physical pain, or mental health issues like depression, anger, and anxiety. Our body responds to our emotional state and reacts accordingly. You deserve so much better than that. You already suffered once, why continue to suffer over and over again. LET IT GO.

Choosing to forgive is spiritually cleansing. Everyone talks about detoxing. Spiritually detoxing includes forgiveness. Depending on how severe the matter is, it may take time to let it go, but throughout this journey I will guide you through how to truly let go and maintain your healing. Life is too short to be ill (mentally or physically) over something that happened months, years, or even decades ago. As you go through this journey of forgiveness, I want to make sure you are building your foundation of healing with the appropriate mindset and spiritual posture. I challenge you to release the tightly gripped pain you are carrying from your past, so that you can widely stretch out your hands to receive what God has for you. Choosing to forgive will help you to grow stronger spiritually and physically.

Challenge

Make a list of the things you want to let go of. This is a process, so as you think of more things continue to add them to the list.

Prayer

Heavenly Father, help me to posture my hands in a way that allows me to receive what you have for me. Show me the things from my past that I still hold on to and help me to release it to you. Guide me in this spiritual detox, so I can come out with a pure heart and a clear mind. In Jesus name, Amen.

Day 5

Misconceptions of Forgiveness

"Do not conform to the pattern of this world, but be transformed by the renewing of your mind. Then you will be able to test and approve what God's will is — his good, pleasing and perfect will."
- Romans 12:2

"You don't need to forgive," or "The other person does not deserve your forgiveness." These are the types of messages I see posted as I scroll through social media. It poses the question, why should I forgive when society says it is useless? As I talk to different people of various ages, I realize that many people have misconceptions about what forgiveness is. Some of us have intentionally walked away from the perfect will of God because it does not meet society's definition of "cool." Your journey through forgiveness is very intimate. It's between you and God. Do not let society keep you in bondage. The goal of forgiveness is to aid you in letting go of ill emotions and bondage that occurred from an incident. This means that you do not have to rekindle the relationship, but instead you should pray on it. Some people are just toxic and you don't need that in your life. There may also be relationships that God wants you to mend. Let God lead you in that. I know closure is very important, it was important to me. I allowed not having it to delay my process of forgiveness as I sought closure for something the person could never give me closure for. Sometimes you may get closure from the other person, sometimes you will not. Understand that because you have God in your corner, He is so mighty that He can heal you either way. Let God unfold this for you, because when you try to force closure sometimes you hurt yourself even more.

Another misconception is this notion of "forgive and forget." Please be mindful of this because when you simply forgive and forget, you are also putting yourself in a position to be hurt again. I know you see the best in the person, but you have to view that person holistically. God revealed whatever He revealed to you for a reason. It was for your protection, so forgive and set healthy boundaries that work for you. Forgiveness is not easy, but it is worth it. It does not happen in one day, but over the course of time. Some incidents took me years to forgive because there were so many things that occurred. Healing is a process. God takes His time with you. You are not alone. At any time while reading this if you feel you would like professional assistance like pastoral counseling or therapy, seek the help. It does not make you less of a Christian. God created these professions for a reason. Remember there are many benefits to forgiveness like being able to create healthier relationships, improving mental health, lowering blood pressure, improving self-esteem, and so much more. When you begin to feel overwhelmed and you're not sure if you want to go through this journey, remember the benefits that forgiveness will give you. You deserve the best version of you, and this is why this journey is very crucial beloved.

Lastly, be mindful of who you surround yourself with during this season. Surround yourself with people that uplift you as you go through this. Having a support system will make the process a little easier.

Challenge

Identify the misconceptions you may have about forgiveness, then pray that God will help you have an open mind during this journey.

Prayer

Dear God, help me to yield to my own desires during this process. Lord I want to fully trust you. Help me to remain focused on you and not society or the people around me. Show me the misconceptions I may have regarding forgiveness and help me to properly heal and let go. In Jesus name, Amen.

Day 6

Identifying Where It Hurts

"The righteous cry out, and the LORD hears them; he delivers them from all their troubles."

- Psalms 34:17

In my own personal journey God revealed where it still hurts by having various people pop up in my dreams, through messages, or even by bumping into them in real life. The following exercise is something I would like you to ponder on. It will give you the blueprint you need to start letting go of any ill emotions you may still be holding on to.

Make a list of all the people that have hurt you. Really meditate on it. The hurt can be as simple as calling you names or as complex as abuse and neglect. It does not matter how "big or small" it may seem. If it hurt, it hurt. This part of the exercise is important because it will allow you to really reflect on where it hurts and who hurt you. In order to really forgive and have peace in the present, you must release the demons in your past, this includes your hurt, pain, and traumas. This list may be long, and some people and incidents may come to mind later, and that is okay. This exercise is something I still practice because forgiveness is a continuous thing. Trust me, God has been testing my forgiveness because I am still bumping into people that have done me wrong. I don't even remember some people's names- I just remember the actions, and that is okay too. It is all part of the healing process, take your time. Hurt is inevitable. All of us will get hurt every now and then. God did not promise that life was going to be easy, but He promised that we would not be alone in the fight and that He would supply our every need according to His will. Healing does not always feel good, and neither does forgiveness, but it is worth it. Anything that is worth having is worth fighting for; and peace of mind is definitely a valuable asset.

Challenge

Review the list you began working on in Day 4 and continue adding anything that comes to mind no matter how big or small the offense. Also think about how the offense made you feel.

Prayer

Heavenly Father, please show me where it still hurts. Show me the places that I chose to suppress because the pain is so intense. Slowly walk me through this process and let me know that you are here, and I am not alone in this journey. You are a great Father and an amazing healer. In Jesus name, Amen.

Day 7

It's Time to Heal

"Now the Lord is the Spirit, and where the Spirit of the Lord is, there is freedom." – 2 Corinthians 3:17

Now that you have created a list of people that hurt you, we can move on to the next step in the exercise. Remember, you can do this exercise as many times as you need to because forgiveness is an ongoing process.

Use this saying as you fill in the blanks with each name you placed on your list. "I choose to forgive [insert name] for [state what they did]. Which made me feel [express how it made you feel]. I no longer want to hold these ill emotions. I choose to release it to you God."

Here is an example. I choose to forgive [my father] for [not being there for me the majority of my life]. His not being there made me feel [worthless and alone]. I no longer want to hold these ill emotions. I choose to release it to you God.

You can write this down or verbalize it. Either way, identify the action and the person that hurt you. Release the ill emotions you are holding in, which will take away the power of the matter. I literally felt lighter after doing this exercise a few times.

The beautiful thing about the God we serve is that He does not want you to hold on to this baggage. He loves you enough to take it from you, but you have to trust Him enough to release it. When you do this exercise the first time, you may not feel any different. Keep doing it until you feel like you have let it go. Every time you get upset with the person, do it again and again until you feel like you have let it go. Holding on to the matter will continue to give it power over you, but releasing it to a loving God will shift the dynamic and give God the power. Doing this breaks bondage and allows you to live in freedom.

Challenge

Take your time and begin practicing the exercise shared. Do it as many times as you need to.

Prayer

Dear Lord, as I practice this exercise I pray you would make yourself present. Meet me where I am and help me to feel the release of the baggage I am finally choosing to let go. I want to feel true joy, peace, and freedom. In the name of Jesus, Amen.

Day 8

How Do I Know If I Forgave?

"Do not let any unwholesome talk come out of your mouths, but only what is helpful for building others up according to their needs, that it may benefit those who listen. And do not grieve the Holy Spirit of God, with whom you were sealed for the day of redemption. Get rid of all bitterness, rage and anger, brawling and slander, along with every form of malice. Be kind and compassionate to one another, forgiving each other, just as in Christ God forgave you."

— Ephesians 4:29-32

How do you know if you have really forgiven? This is a question I am often asked. Just imagine the person that hurt you walked into the room right now. Really close your eyes and imagine them walking into the room. I want you to pay attention to your initial reaction. How did you feel? Did you feel anger, rage, sad, scared, or anxious? Did you purposely avoid the person? What thoughts popped into your head? If your thoughts were negative, this is a sign of unforgiveness. This scenario is an example of how unforgiveness steals power from you by giving it to the person that hurt you. No one should have the ability to take your joy by simply walking into the room. At that point, you have given that person way too much power. This is a warning sign. When the Bible speaks about the joy that the world cannot give or take away, it is true. Again, unforgiveness is a silent thief. You will find yourself giving away things you never noticed was taken. The way to regain your authority is by being transparent. Be transparent with God when discussing the pain and the hurt you have endured. He already knows how you feel before you speak it. But just like any other relationship, He wants you to communicate with Him. God will show you where it hurts, you just have to pay attention to the signs and be willing to go through the forgiveness process with Him. The process will look different for each relationship.

Here is another scenario to ponder. What would you do if God told you to minister to the person that hurt you? What would be your initial response? Just this year I was late to church. When I walked in they were singing my song, so I immediately went into worship and found the closest seat next to me. During this service the pastor instructed us to grab our neighbor's hand and pray for them. I looked over at my neighbor and to my surprise it was a person that had really done me wrong at a former job by trying to get me fired. I had not spoken to him since that day, which had been years prior. God was really testing my forgiveness. I was hesitant to grab his hand, but God started dealing with me. He encouraged me to be the light in the darkness. I did not want to be like Jonah in the Bible and deliberately block someone's blessings or prayer because I had stuff I was holding on to. God told me to let it go and I did. You do not know how your lack of forgiveness can be holding someone back from what God has for them or maybe even what God has for you. Let it go, so you can be obedient to God's perfect will.

Challenge

Close your eyes and imagine each person on your list is coming through the door one by one. Be honest and transparent with yourself about your initial reaction to each person. If it is anything negative, go back to Challenge 7 and try that exercise again. If you have to do this, don't feel bad. Remember, forgiveness and healing are a process. It takes time. You got this!

Prayer

Mighty God, help me to be mindful of the way I live. Guide my mouth and thoughts so that only words that are pleasing to you come to mind. Help me to understand that your purpose for my life is greater than just me. Remove the selfish or ill feelings that I may have, so that I can follow your perfect will and be an example of your unconditional love regardless of how hard it may be. In Jesus name, Amen.

Day 9

Layers to Forgiveness

"The righteous person may have many troubles, but the Lord delivers him from them all."
— Psalm 34:19

Oftentimes when people think of forgiveness, they think of just forgiving the individual that has hurt them. That is definitely a start, but God showed me through this journey that this is just the first layer of the "forgiveness onion." There are so many layers to forgiveness that God will continue to peel piece by piece until you get to the core of the matter. He cannot just start you at the core because it will be more than you can handle. This is why forgiveness is a continuous area that we all can work on. God knows how much we can bare, so He pulls back a layer at a time. Sometimes it takes numerous attempts to forgive the same situation. You can forgive the person and still feel some type of way about a particular action. I caught myself being anxious when expressing my emotions to my significant other due to lack of forgiveness and healing from previous relationships that had nothing to do with my current relationship. This was rooted in my lack of forgiveness from a former spouse's actions. God was showing me that I still had more layers to peel.

A great starting point is typically forgiving the person that hurt you, then you work on forgiving the actual action. This does not always happen all at one time. I have also realized that after forgiving the person and the action, sometimes we can harbor unforgiveness for other people we feel were involved.

Prime example, just last year I thought I was over a traumatic situation I had experienced until I ran into the person's brother. I went into a sudden panic attack because I was overwhelmed with anxiety. I had to go into another room and regroup. The guy's brother was there when the situation happened and did not help me, so I had to forgive the brother too. Honestly, I had forgotten all about the brother, but I had to run into him to know that it was still a sensitive area for me. God knows what we can handle. This was another layer that was peeled from me. You will not know how many layers there are to peel until God reveals the matter to you. Pay attention to your emotions and the people that you run into during this journey. God may be trying to peel back the next layer. Take your time in your healing journey and God will continue to show you the places where it hurts. Trust Him and know that forgiveness leads to true freedom.

Challenge

Make a chart with "person, action, feeling and people associated" as the labels. Take offenses from the list you created and add them to the chart. The person will be the person who offended you. The action is what occurred to offend you. The feeling is how the event made you feel, and lastly the people associated are the people that were around that may have contributed to the offense by what they said, and did or did not do. This will help you identify the different layers of forgiveness and what you need to forgive.

Prayer

Gracious God, you know how much I can bear. As you continue to pull back layers of pain and bondage, help me to feel the release and freedom that follows. Help me to renew my mind so I do not fall into the same traps again. Thank you for being with me and being the great protector that you are. In Jesus name, Amen.

Day 10

Learning How to Cope

"So do not fear, for I am with you; do not be dismayed, for I am your God. I will strengthen you and help you; I will uphold you with my righteous right hand." — Isaiah 41:10

When I was younger I would get random cuts and bruises. Whenever I would show my mother the cut, she would take me into the bathroom, pull out the alcohol, and I would immediately panic because I knew it was going to hurt. In a calming voice she would tell me the importance of cleaning the wound before putting a band-aid on it.

Sometimes walking through forgiveness and healing can be very challenging. To be completely honest, sometimes it hurts even worse than the initial wound. It will burn, and its' going to hurt, but like the alcohol it is cleansing you and washing away the impurities. It is growing pains. These growing pains are going to elevate you to the next level. Just like my mother comforted me when I became afraid of the cleansing portion, God is an amazing Father and healer, He will guide you and comfort you through the pain as well. Remember when you are weak, that is really when you are strong because you have an undefeatable God in your corner. In the mist of feeling the emotion, it is important that you identify positive coping skills that you can use to aid you through your healing when it gets tough.

What do you like to do? As an adult this is often a hard question to answer. Think about when you were a child. Did you like watching movies, being outside in nature, listening to music, cooking, gardening, reading a book, talking to someone that genuinely cares, writing? Of course, some of these activities may have to be modified as an adult, but it helps you in understanding things you genuinely like. Every coping skill may not work in that moment because different coping skills serve different purposes. For example, watching a funny movie may take your mind off the matter if it is becoming too stressful, while writing may help you to release some ill emotions. Both coping skills are healthy, just be mindful of what coping skill best fits you in the moment. You have to consistently be mindful of your feelings during this process. Prayer is always a great coping skill, but sometimes we have to pair it with other things. If you are feeling overwhelmed with negative emotions while going through this process, take breaks and do something that will take your mind off the matter. If you feel like you are going to explode with emotions do something POSITIVE that will help you release the emotion like writing, talking to someone you trust, or exercising. Also keep in mind, if you feel your emotions are becoming hard to manage, you can always seek professional or pastoral counseling as well.

Challenge

Make a list of positive coping skills you can use to help you during this challenge.

Prayer

God, help me to be aware of my emotions and what I need during my healing journey. Help me to find positive coping skills that I can use to aid me through this challenging time. Surround me with people that I can trust and shower me with your love. In Jesus name, Amen.

Day 11

In My Feelings

"And after you have suffered a little while, the God of all grace, who has called you to his eternal glory in Christ, will himself restore, confirm, strengthen, and establish you." – 1 Peter 5:10

Sitting in your emotions is vital as you go through your healing process. As humans we struggle to sit in our emotions typically for one or two reasons. The first reason is typically distorted thinking. You may feel that sitting in your emotions will not help or that it is a sign of weakness. The second reason is because if you sit in your emotions for too long you may become engulfed by them. When I say sit in your emotions, I want you to do it in moderation. If you feel like crying, cry! Do not hold it in. There are many benefits to crying. It helps release tension and stress. If you feel like you are feeling ill emotions too deeply, take a break using appropriate coping skills whether it is seeking professional help, watching a movie, or taking a walk. This is also why it is important to know what coping skills are most helpful for you.

Today's topic is a challenge to refrain from suppressing what you feel. Release them in a healthy manner. I like to think of emotions like a thermostat.

You should typically be room temperature, but if you feel yourself getting too hot or cold this is an indication that something is wrong. God is trying to show you something, so as you recollect your past and seek to forgive you have to feel that pain. This is often why people do not want to go through the healing process, because they are afraid of feeling the pain. But honestly, by not going through it you are still feeling the pain. Healing is like surgery. If someone told you that you had cancer in your body, what would you do? Would you undergo surgery to remove the cancer, or would you ignore it? The choice is yours; and there is pain in both choices. If you choose to get surgery, you may feel pain during the surgery and maybe for a period of time afterwards, but once it is out of your body you will have peace of mind. Choosing to ignore the cancer is painful because it eventually spreads and starts affecting other areas of your body. Ouch! The cancer (unsettled pain) will spread into your relationships, work, marriage, sobriety, YOUR PURPOSE, YOUR CONNECTION WITH GOD, and so much more! In order to get the healing we so desperately want, we have to journey through the feelings that come along with it. This means sitting in the emotion and allowing yourself to feel the sadness or the anger in moderation. It is okay to not be okay. It is okay to be hurt or heartbroken, but you have to be real with yourself. You cannot ignore the emotion, suppress it, or numb it because ultimately you are delaying your own healing process. If you numbed your heart to certain situations, you may have to ask God to soften your heart to the situation again. Sit in the emotion, but do not let it engulf you. When feeling the emotion too deeply, you can easily lose focus of the original purpose of the journey, which is healing. Just know that if you continue to pursue the journey with God, He will lead you to restoration, confirmation, strength, and establishment.

Challenge

As you go through the day, be aware of the emotions you feel. Take time at the end of the day, really reflect on the different emotions you experienced. Pay attention to what you allowed yourself to feel and what you suppressed. Also take notes of the emotions that you may have felt for a longer period of time.

Prayer

Lord, let me know that I am not alone when sitting in my emotions. Shower me with your love and mercy. Give me the strength that I need to go through this and the wisdom I need to appropriately use positive coping skills and support. Give me a glimpse of what is to come if I continue going through this forgiveness journey with you. In Jesus name, Amen.

Day 12

Keeping It Real

"God is our safe place and our strength. He is always our help when we are in trouble."
— Psalms 46:1

What is in that dark room that you keep locked hoping no one goes into? That situation or thing you pretend never existed, so you stuff it in your closet to hide it from the world. That is the thing I want you to reflect on while reading this text today. One of the things that challenged me the most during my healing process was "calling it what it is." I had trained myself to numb my pain and emotions. People did not know I was hurting because I was able to mask my hurt so well. I could talk about my past hurts and not even change my emotion. I could walk past a person that had hurt me and show no emotions. I was emotionally numb, and thought this made life easier for me. I thought this meant I was good. I even tricked myself into believing that maybe I was not hurting at all. Until one day, God really called me out.

Being transparent is hard because you have to admit what really happened. I was able to live with some of the traumas I had been through for quite some time because I was in denial and had never admitted the things I had been through, not even to myself. I was not transparent about how I felt. I was not honest with myself. I had been in an abusive situation, and I never called it for what it was. I would just say it was toxic, or sometimes not acknowledge it at all. The first time I was able to call it for what it was, I broke down. I was terrified because I had never had a mental breakdown. After breaking down, I felt somewhat free. I was able to be honest with myself and that was a different experience for me. That was the moment God could really heal me because I was being honest with myself and honest with Him. I had finally opened the door to that room that no one was allowed to enter. God was able to do something with my transparency. He was able to heal me. There is power in calling it what it is.

When we go through situations, sometimes we minimize what occurs so that we can feel less pain and put on this unrealistic persona like everything is okay when everything is not. The first step in overcoming a situation is admitting that you have a problem. You have to be realistic with yourself. The only way God can heal it, is if you call it by name. I let shame and fear keep me in bondage for so many years. I was ashamed of what happened. Do not allow shame, guilt, fear, or whatever ill emotion you are holding on to, hold you back from letting go. Gone are the days that we are ashamed or guilty. Healing is more important. You serve a God that sees all, knows all, and still chooses to love you unconditionally. He is a safe place and most importantly, your supernatural strength. He is your superpower. There is no need to hold back from Him. Use your God given voice, walk in your authority and call it by name.

Challenge

Today, take time to really journal your true feelings about a particular event, person, or situation. If you notice yourself beginning to feel extreme emotions, complete one of the coping skills you put on the list in challenge 10 or talk to someone you trust.

Prayer

Dear Father, you know the things I try to mask and hide. You know where I am still hurting. Help me to be honest with myself and you so I can let go of the pain and the hurt. Show me the areas that I have deceived myself in possibly thinking I am okay when I am actually still hurting. Remove the shame, guilt, or any other ill feeling that is holding me back from being transparent with you. Help me to release these emotions, so I can experience true peace. In Jesus name, Amen.

Day 13

Don't Take It Personal

"Very truly I tell you Pharisees, anyone who does not enter the sheep pen by the gate, but climbs in by some other way, is a thief and robber. The one who enters by the gate is the shepherd of the sheep. The gatekeeper opens the gate for him, and the sheep listen to his voice. He calls his own sheep by name and leads them out."
- John 10:1-3

When you went into that dark place after your tragedy happened, what emotions did you internalize? Did you feel like you were unloved, damaged goods, unworthy? No, really think about this and dig deep. Oftentimes we internalize negative aspects from past occurrences we endured. Internalizing the negative actions that have been done to us affects the way we view ourselves, which then impacts our ability to make healthy decisions because we are making decisions to keep ourselves from getting hurt again. Now we are not acting out of love (which is God's desire for us), we are acting out of survival or defense. There is a difference. Nonetheless, our decision making affects the way we treat the people around us. It is a domino effect, which then trickles down to the people we encounter.

Choosing not to heal and forgive can cause you to internalize baggage that does not belong to you. That extra baggage can put a strain on your relationship with God. It seems so easy to "move on" leaving the past locked up in the "dark" closet no one knows about. You can only hide it for so long, but what happens when people begin to notice that dark closet. It is like putting clean clothes on top of smelly clothes. After a while all the clothes are going to stink. The concept is the same for unhealed wounds. You can pretend like they do not exist, but everyone smells it (especially depending on how deep the cut is). These negative core beliefs that were created from your hurt and traumas were never from God. The devil uses these things to keep you from God, your purpose, healing, and overcoming. The devil wants to keep you in bondage, chained up to your past. Listening to the enemy will lead you further into darkness. You have more power than you think. You have to renounce these lies from the enemy. The first step is acknowledging the negative thoughts. The next step is challenging the negative thoughts with the truth (God's Word). For example, if you had a thought like "I shouldn't try this, I am not good enough." Well, who said I am not good enough? Challenge the thought. In Psalm 139:14, God tells me I am fearfully and wonderfully made (speak God's Word).

You have to know who is speaking. If what is being said is condemning or making you feel bad, that is not God.

If the thought is not referring you back to scripture, it is probably a robber trying to climb over the gate. God's love is unconditional regardless of what you have done or gone through. When God speaks, He speaks out of love. When God opens the gates, He calls you by name. He speaks to who you were created to be. He does not shame you for who you were. God's sheep know His voice. Nonetheless, whatever negative thoughts enter your mind from past events, find Bible verses you can use to challenge the devil and speak truth into your life. Remember the TRUTH will set you free.

Challenge

Make a list identifying the negative things you internalized from your trauma or offense. Next to that column make a list of the positive traits you have, who you are striving to become and who God says you are.

Prayer

Dear God, reveal any lies I have chosen to hold on to regarding my past hurt. Show me where these lies have distorted my view of myself. Aid me in regaining the godly confidence and authority that you have given me because I am your child. Help me to see the person you created me to be. In Jesus name, Amen.

Day 14

Forgiving God

"You keep track of all my sorrows. You have collected all my tears in your bottle. You have recorded each one in your book." - Psalms 56:8

Have you ever wondered why you had to endure the struggles, traumas, and trials that you faced in life? Have you ever wondered why God would allow certain things to happen to you? Have you ever thought how can I believe in something like this? It is unfair and unfortunate what happened to you. The human side of us wants to blame our misfortunes on someone and sometimes we make God our target, but we have to understand that God and life are not the same. God did not tell us that our journey through life would be simple. Jesus said in John 16:33, *"I have told you all this so that you may have peace in me. Here on earth you will have many trials and sorrows. But take heart, because I have overcome the world."*

Jesus is telling us that we WILL have many trials and sorrows. We are going to go through some things here on earth and sometimes it may hurt. Jesus did not sugar coat anything, but He ends on a positive note encouraging us to stay focused because He HAS OVERCOME THE WORLD. God loved you enough to allow His son to die for you, so that He could have a deeper relationship with you. So when your pain seems hard to bear, know that He has never left you. Know that He will be your strength. Know that you will overcome these trials and tribulations because your Father has paved the way for you. You have to shift your perspective. The devil's goal is to distract you and make you think less of God and yourself. Do not let him trick you into thinking less of God. God gives everyone free will. Understand that when anything ill happened to you, God did not just turn the other direction. He did not ignore you or leave you. He cried with you. He was beside you. His heart was broken too. The scripture states that God keeps track of all of our sorrows. He has collected all your tears in a bottle. Why would God do this? Because He took those offenses personally. Just like everyone has free will, you also have to remember that everyone will be held accountable for their actions. Do not think there is not a consequence for the person's actions. Please understand that when it is time, God will rectify it, not you. God has a way of turning tragedies into fortunes and broken people into masterpieces. He will take the tears that He collected and use them to water His plans for you, but if you are holding offenses towards God, it puts a strain on your relationship and makes life seem foggy and dark. Clear up your vision by releasing it in prayer. A good thing about walking with God in overcoming the matter is that He will grow you, elevate you, and use you to reach others that have been in similar situations. Everything is working for your good beloved, just make sure you are keeping your vision clear by trusting the Lord.

Challenge

Make a list of the times you felt like God was not there, and then ask God to help give you closure around what happened. Ask Him to reveal His purpose or what you were supposed to learn from that situation. He will reveal Himself, but you have to be open to receiving the closure He gives you.

Prayer

Dear Heavenly Father, I have pondered over my perceived offenses, and I wanted to tell you I am sorry. Reveal to me any ill feelings that are hindering our relationship. Please come into my heart and heal those unsettling feelings that I may have towards you. Fill them with your everlasting love. Help me to bind up the lies of the enemy and fill them with your truth. In Jesus name, Amen.

Day 15

Learning to Forgive Myself

"But he said to me, "My grace is sufficient for you, for my power is made perfect in weakness." Therefore I will boast all the more gladly of my weaknesses, so that the power of Christ may rest upon me." - 2 Corinthians 12:9

One of the most heartfelt moments I ever had was with a nine-year old girl. I was driving her and her sisters to Vacation Bible School. We had a casual conversation and then it got quiet for a while. She was looking out the window. Her voice softened and she said, "Ms. Tiana." And I said, "Yes honey." She paused as if she was in deep thought and continued, "I have done some really bad things in life." She paused again, then looked at me with tears in her eyes and said, "Does God still love me?" I was quiet for a moment because that very question touched my heart. I told her "Well sweetie, God sees everything. There is nothing you can do to make Him ever stop loving you. He loved you the same today, yesterday, and the day you were born. There is nothing you can do to keep Him from seeking you. You are His child, and His love is unconditional for you." To this day, this story still makes me cry because as an adult how many times have we had the same thoughts, questions, and feelings of uncertainty? How many times does the thought of our wrongdoing haunt us and keep us in bondage, making us want to stray from our relationship with God because we are unsure of His unconditional love for us? The devil likes to play with our areas of ignorance. The previous challenges encouraged you to forgive others and any "perceived" hurt from God. Now we are moving on to the next step in your healing journey, self-forgiveness. This step requires you to look in the mirror and forgive that person in your reflection. This step encourages you to look at the raw version of you- all of your flaws, self-doubt, the things that make you uncomfortable, and the things you never told anyone, those things. These things are rooted in some weakness and hurt from your past. The previous choices you made were done from a broken place, whether it was saying mean things, doing hurtful things, or maybe failing to put yourself first. God wants to unroot those things, but you have to be willing to go there. It is in that place that you will be able to overcome the negative perception that you have of yourself and self-forgiveness can begin.

I picked 2 Corinthians 12:9 as the scripture for today's challenge because it talks about God's grace. God's grace is sufficient, meaning that it does not matter what you have done in the past, God's grace oversees that. His grace is greater than that. As long as you are willing to change for the better, God will remove the blemishes of your past and make you anew. His love is unconditional. If God almighty can look past your flaws and mistakes, then who are you to tear yourself down because of them? If God can love you for who you are right now in this very moment, then why can't you choose to love yourself? In this very moment, I want you to let go of the negative thoughts and hurt regarding you. Choose to forgive the person you see in the mirror. You are not unlovable, you are just hurting. Allow God to show you what He sees in you.

Challenge

Pull the list of positive characteristics you listed in challenge 13. Look at yourself in the mirror and say, "I am" before every positive characteristic. I want you to look yourself in the eyes and declare those positive statements like you mean it. Continue to practice this every day. Even if you don't feel like you believe it, speak it into existence!

Prayer

Gracious God, thank you for your sufficient grace and unconditional love. Please reveal to me the areas that I still have not healed from so I can learn how to forgive and love myself the way you love me. Show me how to unroot habits, mindsets, and attitudes that continue to keep me in bondage. In Jesus name, Amen.

Day 16

See What God Sees

"The son said to him, 'Father, I have sinned against heaven and against you. I am no longer worthy to be called your son.' "But the father said to his servants, 'Quick! Bring the best robe and put it on him. Put a ring on his finger and sandals on his feet." - Luke 15:21-22

One of the most heartfelt lessons I had with God is when he began showing me how He views me. This was a struggle for me; and is something that I consistently have to work on. Pain that had occurred in my past caused me to look at life from a broken lens. I made many mistakes due to viewing things from a broken perspective, some of which caused my heart to hurt even more than before. If I can be completely honest, not only did I allow the pain to alter my viewpoint on life, but I also allowed it to influence my view of myself. At times I did not want to look in the mirror because I was unsure of who I was becoming. I would think things like, "Why would God want someone that is so broken?" My broken lens played a major role in my self-esteem. I could only see my mistakes and the hurt from my past. As a result, I ended up walking on self-inflicted thorns instead of God's smooth path. I endured situations and circumstances that were not necessarily in God's original plan for me. But God is so gracious, He made room for my errors. Not only does He make room, but He will even use those errors to elevate you so you can reach other people. We have to keep in mind that we are children of God, and the world does not define us, neither do our mistakes. Self-love and forgiveness begin with knowing who we are in Christ, and knowing that God loves us and calls us royalty despite what the world says. This is not because you earned it, but because His grace is greater than our mistakes. God looks at you and only sees the person He intends for you to be. He knows that even with a little dirt on your crown, He can easily take the proper soap and rag and wash away your blemishes. This is why the story of the prodigal son in Luke 15:11-24 is so fitting.

In this scripture we find a son who decides to take his portion of his father's estate and leave town. The son blows all of his money and is too ashamed to come back home. He was so deep in his mess that he went to work in a field feeding pigs. He did not have any money, so he would also eat the pigs' food. Imagine how low his self-esteem was at this time. Look at how far sin had taken him away from where God had called him to be. In this verse he expresses that he did not feel like he was worthy enough to be called "son." How often do we feel like this? Finally, the son came home, and his father celebrated his return with open arms. He put a robe, ring, and sandals on him to let him know who he is! Despite the dirt that was on him, he was still his child. The same is true for you. No matter what negative things you may feel about yourself, you will always be God's child. He will always accept you with welcoming arms and will present His best for you to let you know that you are His child. You are royalty, valuable, and loved in His eyes. This is what God sees when he looks at you, crowned one.

Challenge

First ask God, "What do you see when you look at me?" Then close your eyes and begin to picture yourself being washed clean from all the mistakes of your past. Imagine God giving you a beautiful garment to wear and placing a crown on your head. Continue the daydream until you are ready for it to end, but keep it positive.

Prayer

Loving Father, thank you for loving me despite my past pain and mistakes. Thank you for welcoming me with open arms and unconditional love. Help me to see the wonderful qualities that you chose for me. Continue to guide me through my healing and help me to forgive and love myself in the process of this journey. In Jesus name, Amen.

Day 17

Taking Responsibility

"Whoever conceals his transgressions will not prosper, but he who confesses and forsakes them will obtain mercy." – Proverbs 28:13

Today's challenge encourages you to look at the matters that happened and reflect on things that maybe you could have done differently. I know you are probably thinking, what? I was the victim, they did me wrong. And this may very well be true. But taking a look at your actions or red flags you may have seen before can help you grow as a person and learn from the situation, so you are less likely to face the matter again. I am not going to lie, taking responsibility can be hard, especially when some of your choices may have negatively impacted your well-being. As humans we want someone to blame, but how much of that responsibility is yours? Taking ownership of your wrongs is the mature thing to do. I know that in my own traumas, some of them could have been avoided if I had just listened to what God was telling me. Every situation is different. For example, you cannot help who you were born too, so that may not apply. But other situations like getting into that relationship (casual or romantic) or going over to that person's house when you know that God was telling you not to, are examples of matters that may apply to this teaching. In the healing journey, you have to be honest with yourself. Failure to do so can lead to you going right back into the same tragic situation because you failed to accept the part that you can change. God gives us warning before things happen, because He loves us and wants to protect us. When we fail to pay attention to the warning signs in front of our faces, we walk out of God's protection and into the fire. God's Word teaches us God's will and expectations. God sets boundaries with us, but it is our job to listen and take heed. Do not second guess what God is telling you because you may end up walking into the fire. God will allow you to go through the same lesson over and over and over again until you learn the lesson. He is not going to let you skip a grade until you earn it. How many times are you going to have to repeat the same test, when all you have to do is accept your part in the matter and change it for the future? Take time today to reflect on some of the warning signs you missed in the past, so you can make sure that you do not fall into the same trap again in the present or future. Do not get caught up in victimizing yourself, because you are only holding yourself deeper in bondage. Your perspective is so important. When you tell yourself you are the victim, you continue to find ways to fulfill this prophecy. Instead shift your perspective to someone that is a victor and who has overcome the matter, because let's be honest, you are reading this right? So that means you are still here. You are victorious! Take responsibility for the portion that may belong to you, learn from it, forgive yourself and then shift your perspective on the matter.

Challenge

Look over your list of offenses and identify what responsibilities you may have had in them. Then begin to think of ways you can learn from them, so that it does not happen again.

Prayer

Father, there may have been times that I did not listen to your warnings, and I ended up getting myself hurt. Help me to be honest with myself, so that I can learn from my mistakes and in return become closer to you. Thank you for your everlasting love. In Jesus name, Amen.

Day 18

The Kiss of Judas

"While he was still speaking a crowd came up, and the man who was called Judas, one of the Twelve, was leading them. He approached Jesus to kiss him, but Jesus asked him, "Judas, are you betraying the Son of Man with a kiss?"

– Luke 22:47-48

The greatest love story ever is Jesus dying on the cross for us. When Jesus died, He was able to conquer death, save us from sin, and live eternally. His death is a symbol of hope, life, and so much more to God's people. In order for Jesus to have such an amazing testimony, He had to go through a test. He had to face hardships despite the fact that He was perfect. Jesus had to be betrayed in order to die on the cross for our sins. Oftentimes when we reflect on Judas's betrayal, we often think of him as a bad person. But let's be honest, somebody had to do it. The fact of the matter is, although Judas's intentions were not pure, God was still able to use that situation for His glory. God is always in control, and He will use a situation that is "supposed" to be bad to bless you. My question to you is, "Who betrayed you? Who gave you the kiss of Judas?" Although the situation may have caused you pain and heartache, guess what, you are reading this book so that means you made it through. You overcame the matter because God has a plan for your life! You have purpose, you have a calling and God is going to use this matter to bring you closer to where He is trying to take you. You suffered enough. It is time to change your perspective. Imagine if Jesus had spent His time focusing on the fact that Judas betrayed Him, or how people did not accept Him, were rude to Him, and talked about Him, or the physical abuse that He went through. I think you get the point. This would have shifted the dynamics of the story. Hearing His story would have been depressing instead of encouraging. It would have made the story about Jesus being the victim instead of Jesus being victorious. The shift in your story comes from healing and forgiving. It does not mean that the offense did not hurt or that what occurred was right, but your perspective on the situation influences how powerful your story is. Once you change your perspective on the matter, God can use you and get the glory out of the situation. God will be able to elevate you to the next level. This is why you cannot get so caught up on the betrayal portion because you will miss the blessings that stemmed from the matter. You will miss what God is trying to do. Yes, you were fired from your job even though you were a good worker, but maybe you were not valued there, so God gave you a better job where the people see your value. Yes, your significant other did you wrong and the relationship did not work out, but maybe you were investing so much time in that relationship that you did not make time for God or yourself. That break up needed to happen so that you could work on valuing yourself. Maybe your significant other could not go where God was trying to take you. You have to remember, beloved, God is always in control. The kiss of Judas is really God signaling to you, "Hey, things are about to change, but elevation is coming!" You have to be able to lean on God's understanding and stop taking things so personal. It had to happen to get you to the next level. Trust the process, God has you.

Challenge

Look over your list of offenses and see if you can identify any benefits that came from the offense. For example, I got fired from my job, but God blessed me with a new job where people appreciate me.

Prayer

God help me to shift my perspective so that I can see the good that comes from my trials and tribulations instead of the bad. Show me the power that my perspective holds and help me to see things from a supernatural perspective instead of just the physical. In Jesus name, Amen.

Day 19

Changing the Lens

"Bless those who persecute you; bless and do not curse." — Romans 12:14

Today we are going to work on seeing things from the other person's perspective. I know this is a hard step and that is why this book is filled with challenges because I want you to grow. You are probably wondering why you should see anything from the perspective of the person who hurt you, and how this will be helpful? The reason is because it takes away the personal offense. As humans, it's normal to see things from our view, but also very limiting, because we only see a portion of the matter. Being able to look at things from a holistic perspective is life changing because you can get a bigger picture of the matter. Let me explain. When you look at things from another person's perspective, you are able to understand where they are coming from and why they may have made the choice they made. Doing this does not excuse the person's behavior, but it will help you put things into perspective. It is easy to feel like you have been through the most pain and no one can relate. However, the truth is you are not the only person that has endured pain. People act the way they act because it is a learned behavior or a defense mechanism from previous life experiences. For example, if your mother was not the best mother, what was her childhood like? If it was not the best, then it makes sense why she chose the same route because that is what she is used to. It does not make it right and does not take away from your pain, but it does help you to understand that this was not something done to you because you are you, but because she is broken. The truth is we have expectations we expect people to meet and when they do not meet them, we often times become offended and take it personal. Maybe your mother tried her best. Maybe she tried to give you what she felt was best for you at the time, but because of the expectation you had, you felt like she did not meet the bar. She was not able to give you what you felt like you deserved due to her not knowing how. You have to understand that people make decisions based off of their perspective of what they think is best. Your perspective is created from your life experiences, culture, things you see, and so much more. It may be hard to do this for every situation, but if you have background knowledge on the person it normally makes this a little easier. Even if you do not have background knowledge, understand that there are a lot of broken people in this world. It is definitely challenging for all of us. This is why you are reading this, to aid you in your brokenness. The benefit to being healed is that you can see things from a clearer perspective and be able to guard your heart more effectively. I am not saying you should not have standards, please do. I am just trying to guide you in seeing things from the other person's view because at the end of the day, you are God's child and so are they. Yes, God will give the necessary punishment, but He also looks at the entire picture. Take the challenge even further. Do not curse the person that hurt you, instead pray for them because they are hurting too.

Challenge

Identify areas in your life that challenge you to see things from another person's perspective. Look at your list of offenses and see if you can challenge yourself to see things from anyone on that list's perspective. Again, it doesn't mean it was right, but can you see where they are coming from?

Prayer

Lord, help me to understand the importance of interceding for others. Release any ill feelings I may have towards the people that hurt me so that I can pray for them with a pure heart. I pray that you bless the people that have hurt me. Lord, open their eyes so that they can see that true healing comes from you. Hurt people, hurt people. I want to be healed, so I can go out and help others to heal. In Jesus name I pray, Amen.

Day 20

Trust the Process

"Then Peter came to Jesus and asked, "Lord, how many times shall I forgive my brother or sister who sins against me? Up to seven times?" Jesus answered, "I tell you, not seven times, but seventy-seven times." – Matthew 18:21-22

To this day, I still have dreams about past abusers. I used to wake up shaking because of the fear that was attached to the person in my dreams. I would wake up praying and asking God to take away the fear and to help me forgive them. Healing is a process and is something that has to be maintained. I constantly have to check in with God to see how I am doing with my healing. Healing is like an onion, remember we discussed this on day 9. You are constantly pulling back layers that you may not have known existed. Healing takes time and you may have to forgive the same situation a few times before you actually feel the release. It may feel exhausting, and you may want to give up, but remember that you have also fallen short before.

God makes His expectations clear. When you look up forgiveness in the Bible, numerous scriptures tell us that choosing not to forgive will cause the Lord not to forgive us. How many times have you hurt someone else? How many times have you sinned against God? Imagine if God held the same mentality you have towards others, towards you. That would be depressing right? Matthew 6:14-15 states, *"For if you forgive other people when they sin against you, your heavenly Father will also forgive you. But if you do not forgive others their sins, your Father will not forgive your sins."* We are not perfect, and this is why God encourages us to extend forgiveness to others just like he extends it to us. God tells us that we are to forgive 77 times 7 times PER DAY. Yes, everyday. Our goal is to be like Christ and in the Bible He states that we have to forgive so that God can forgive us.

A lack of forgiveness creates barriers between you and God. When you choose not to forgive you are willingly giving away your God-given authority. You are also taking the risk of not being forgiven yourself. Is it really worth that? You have come too far in your journey to turn around. I know some stuff may have hurt you bad and you are tired, and just want this to be over and to be happy. How deeply the person hurt you will determine the number of layers required to peel back. God will walk with you through this journey, and He will never put more on you than you can bear. But you cannot give up, you have to keep pushing! The enemy wants you to give up. He wants you to feel like this is worthless. You have so much to lose if you become discouraged now. You have made so much progress.

Even if it seems little, it is still progress. If you have deleted a toxic person's number, that is progress. If you no longer hold ill feelings towards someone, that is progress. If you are praying for someone that hurt you, that is progress. Sometimes we get so caught up in our daily routine that we do not take a moment to appreciate how much we have grown. You can write it down, make a video, or whatever God puts on your heart to keep track of your progress. Doing this will motivate you to keep going, especially on days that do not feel as rewarding. You got this and God has you!

Challenge

Make a list of the progress you have made so far in your forgiveness journey. Celebrate by doing something positive and nice for yourself.

Prayer

Heavenly Father, it is so easy to give up, but thank you for never giving up on me and not allowing me to give up on myself. Thank you for pushing me to be the best that I can be. Help me to see the progress I am making in my healing journey, and let that be encouragement on the days I do not feel like journeying through. You truly are amazing. In Jesus name, Amen.

Day 21

Working Against the Flesh

"So I say, walk by the Spirit, and you will not gratify the desires of the flesh. For the flesh desires what is contrary to the Spirit, and the Spirit what is contrary to the flesh. They are in conflict with each other, so that you are not to do whatever you want."

– Galatians 5:16-17

How do you build a strong healthy relationship with your significant other? Really take a moment and reflect. One of the major factors should be spending quality time, right? So why do you treat your relationship with God different from anyone else you care about. Why do you allow your relationship with God to suffer, while you let worldly things consume your time and energy. Do you really want to take your relationship with God to the next level? Do you really want to see the results of you healing journey? You have to stop being a creature of fleshly habits. If you want to see a breakthrough with your healing, you cannot refuse to take action because you don't feel like it. We are fighting a battle against flesh and spirit. Forgiveness is a choice and an action. God tells us that faith without works is dead. So how can you feel like healing, but not want to do anything to change your situation. You have to break the habit and go against the flesh. The flesh wants you to do what feels natural, but God is supernatural, meaning that we have to exit the natural realm in order to find Him. This means that we have to put in work. Every day we are fighting a supernatural battle, whether you are aware and equipped is another story. The more you feed you flesh, the stronger it will become, and the more you build your spirit, the weaker your flesh becomes. You feed your spirit by building up your relationship with God, seeking Him in scripture and prayer, being intentional with your time with Him, and being persistent. As you continue building your spirit, you will begin to notice that making intentional time with God will become easier.

When times get rough, remember the Bible is right there. Be mindful of the temptations of the flesh. As you begin to pick up the Bible, your flesh may try to tell you, "Not right now." Push through and make time anyways. It's your actions that make all the difference. When you have the urge to go to church all week and then Sunday comes and you want to "sleep in," push through because God is calling you. When you have the urge to harbor ill emotions, push through and ask God to help you forgive. Being a creature of fleshly habits will leave you in the same situation- feeling hurt, exhausted, and alone. Choose to forgive and push through with building your relationship with God regardless of how you feel. As you do this you will begin to see a difference in your life, your perspective, and your relationship with God. This is also how you maintain your healing and peace of mind… by keeping your mind stayed on God.

Challenge

Today, be intentional about the time you spend with God. Think of other ways you can be more intentional with Him, more often.

Prayer

Lord, forgive me for not being intentional when making time for you. I am sorry for putting myself and other things in your place. Show me what fleshly habits I need to let go of and help me to be obedient to the Spirit. Please guide me on how to be intentional with you so that I can build my spirit and weaken my flesh. In Jesus name, Amen.

Day 22

Learning from the Past

"The LORD will make you the head, not the tail. If you pay attention to the commands of the LORD your God that I give you this day and carefully follow them, you will always be at the top, never at the bottom." – Deuteronomy 28:13

Take a second to honestly reflect on your life. If you had to relive your life all over again would you do it? Do you feel like you got the short end of the stick when it comes to life? If I had answered this question before I endured my healing process, I would probably have laughed, and thought, "Of course I don't want to relive some of my traumas." Let's be honest, who would? It seems like when you view things from a broken place, all you can see are the cracks, the things that were bad despite all the good that also occurred.

Reflecting on this question from a more healed perspective (remember healing is a continuous journey), I have some understanding as to why God allowed me to go through certain situations. God opened my eyes and allowed me to see the good that came out of my afflictions. He allowed me to see the authority that He granted me, the wisdom, and a deeper understanding of my purpose which stemmed from my afflictions. My afflictions gave me passion for my purpose. I know I talked about this in the previous challenge, but now I want to take it a step further and talk about how our affliction can bring us closer to our purpose.

When God created you, He had a plan for your life. He created you because He knew that there was something only you could bring into this world and He felt like it was needed. The devil often attacks when we are doing things to fulfill our purpose. The devil's goal is to get you off track. Before I even knew I was a gifted speaker, my 2nd grade teacher tried to encourage my mother to put me in speech therapy. There was nothing wrong with my speech, the devil was just trying to create insecurity in me. Nonetheless, the devil will try to create afflictions around your purpose to make you stray away.

Deliverance ministry is one of my callings. I am consistently serving and helping people break free from bondage, but one of the reasons why I am so effective at helping people is not because of my degrees, but more so because of the situations that I have been through personally. A lot of the things that my clients tell me happened in their life, I have been through as well, so I speak to them from a place of someone who has overcome. My afflictions allow me to be more relatable to others. I know the signs and know how to comfort others that have been through similar situations because I know what I wanted when I endured my own personal situations. My experiences, both the good and bad, made me who I am today. I am not my trauma. I am not a victim. I am not the tail, but I am the head. I am victorious, and the same applies to you. You are so strong. You are so loved. You are very much victorious, and people need to hear your story. Your story will help others to overcome their own demons. But like the scripture says, you have to be obedient. Failure to tell others your story will not only hold you back, but it will hold back the people that God wants to hear your story. You are holding them back from the deliverance that they need. This is why you have to be healed from the matter, so that when you speak, you speak from a whole place, and not a broken one.

Speaking from a broken place will only cause you to bleed on others, which will in turn hurt them, even if your intentions are good. Do not be ashamed of the trials you had to endure. When God tells you to speak on it, do it because you never know whose life you will touch. He wants to uplift you. You conquered it, now lift others up so they can conquer as well.

Challenge

Look over your list of offenses again. What lessons did you learn that you can now teach to others?

Prayer

God, thank you for renewing my mind so I can speak from a whole place instead of a broken one. Thank you for taking situations the devil meant for my bad and turning it around for my good. You said in your Word that as long as I am obedient, I will be the head and not the tail and I want to live that. In Jesus name, Amen.

Day 23

Be Aware of the Red Flags

"For no good tree bears bad fruit, nor again does a bad tree bear good fruit, for each tree is known by its own fruit. For figs are not gathered from thornbushes, nor are grapes picked from a bramble bush. The good person out of the good treasure of his heart produces good, and the evil person out of his evil treasure produces evil, for out of the abundance of the heart his mouth speaks."

– Luke 6:43-45

My mother raised me to say what I mean and mean what I say. If I gave you my word, then I had to follow through. My mom would not let me quit until I did what I said. At an early age this taught me the importance of a person's words and actions. Anyone can tell you what you want to hear, but their actions will ALWAYS show their true intentions. As 1 John 3:18 says, *"Dear children, let us not love with words or speech but with actions and in truth."* Your words and actions have to coincide or there is a problem.

2 Timothy 3:1-5, "People will be lovers of themselves, lovers of money, boastful, proud, abusive, disobedient to their parents, ungrateful, unholy, without love, unforgiving, slanderous, without self-control, brutal, not lovers of the good,

treacherous, rash, conceited, lovers of pleasure rather than lovers of God — having a form of godliness but denying its power. Have nothing to do with such people."

God will not have you out here looking crazy. He will always reveal what needs to be seen. We typically call these red flags, but in the Bible God talks about inspecting the fruit of the Spirit. If you are seeing things like the characteristics shared in the scripture above, this person is showing you that their intentions are impure, so you should be very mindful and prayerful. *If the person has good fruit, you will see things like love, joy, peace, patience, kindness, generosity, faithfulness, gentleness and self-control as evidence of God's work in them (Galatians 5:22–23).* As disciples of Christ, we should model what He showed us here on earth. In order to maintain your healing, you must test the fruit. This is why forgiveness is so important. If you are walking around with a broken lens, you won't be able to see what God is showing you because the cracks in your glasses will distort your vision. Your vision needs to be clear so that you can see the actions and words of the people around you.

As revealed in Luke 6:45, a person will show you who they are in due time by their words and actions. Understand that their actions and words are not a reflection of you, but rather themselves. This is not just in romantic relationships, but every relationship. Pay attention to what that person brings into your life. Trust God enough to know that when He shows you something, He is showing you for your protection. He knows what is going to happen, you just have to be open and obedient. I could have saved myself from so much heartache had I just paid attention to the signs God was showing me. When God gives you a red flag, pray and ask Him what He wants you to do and follow suit.

Challenge

Review your list of offenses. What red flags did you overlook and how can you avoid them next time?

Prayer

Lord, help me to bare the fruit that you bore when you were here on earth. Help me to make sure that my heart, thoughts, words, and actions align with your perfect will. Lord open my eyes so that I can see the signs that you are showing me and give me clear direction on how you want me to handle the matter. Thank you for your protection. In Jesus name, Amen.

Day 24

Detoxing

"Search me, O God, and know my heart! Try me and know my thoughts! And see if there be any grievous way in me, and lead me in the way everlasting!" – Psalm 139:23-24

I went to counseling once, this is when I was trying to figure out how to feel again. I was numb and at the time it seemed like numbing the pain was easier than facing the problem. The counselor was confused at how I was able to share my story in a humorous way with no glimpse of pain. I explained to her that if someone stole your car the first time how would you feel? Devastated. How do you feel after the second, third, seventh time your car is stolen? You start to become desensitized to it. She just stared. Abuse was common in my life from a child to an adult. I found comfort in toxic relationships. When having that conversation with the counselor, I realized that maybe I was not helpless. Maybe I just needed to shift my perspective and break my negative thinking patterns. At that moment I realized just how harmful these thinking patterns were and how I deserved so much better.

Just because something is a norm to you, does not mean that it is healthy. Just because you can bare certain things, does not mean that you should tolerate it. We talked about forgiveness, but this is how you maintain your healing, by breaking negative thinking traps and habits. It is so easy to fall into these habits because it is what we are used too. It becomes an automatic thought, which makes the habit a blind spot for us. It's something we naturally do. We have to constantly be mindful of our thinking patterns and actions. The first step to breaking negative thinking traps and habits is acknowledging when you are engaging in the habits. The devil's goal is to have you running in circles instead of making progress. You will find yourself running into the same situation with different faces over and over, if you don't learn your lesson, so you can progress and not be stagnant. Change can be hard, and it can be scary trying something new because you are not sure of what the outcome will be. You have to have faith that it is better than what you have been through. You have to believe that God desires nothing but the best for you, beloved. You have to love yourself more than the situation, and finally decide that you are more important. You may receive some push back from people that are used to the old you, but when you let God in, you become a new person. God will first begin working on your mind because He knows how influential your thinking habits can be on your well-being. When God shows you a sign, take heed. It will protect you from falling back into broken habits. Know that changing your habits, the people you surround yourself with, thinking patterns, or whatever else God is telling you to change may seem challenging at first, but you have a protector that is walking with you every step of the way. All He asks is that you are obedient. We all fall short, so when you fall down, get back up and grab His hand. We serve a God that is greater than our troubles, burdens, fears, and pain. He will show you how to get out of these thinking traps. He will put positive people in your life that will support you through your journey. It is time for a change. It may seem scary, but God is good, and He will walk you through it if you let Him.

Challenge

What habits or defense mechanisms did you create due to your past hurt? What are some things you can do to break these habits?

Prayer

Father, I want more out of life than the things I choose to settle for. Reveal to me what habits I need to let go of and transform my mind so that I can become more like you. In Jesus name, Amen.

Day 25

Building A Support System

"For where two or three are gathered together in my name, there I am in the midst of them."
— Matthew 18:20

Earlier in the book, I mentioned how I chose to suffer alone. I felt like pain was a sign of weakness. I felt ashamed and embarrassed about some of the problems I had. I felt like my issues were not anyone else's problem. I chose to be silent in the midst of my issues. This is one of the enemy's greatest tactics to make you feel like you are the only one facing your hardships. It isolates you from your loved ones because you feel like you are by yourself. No one will understand, but the truth is that there is nothing new under the sun (Ecclesiastes 1:9). Thus, what you have been through someone else has faced. God did not create us to be alone, but to connect to Him and also to others. It is important for your physical and mental health to utilize your support. How do you define what a positive support is for you? Some people automatically think of their family. In some cases, your family may be a great support system for you. But in other cases, your family may not understand your situation, they may take things personal, or maybe your family is toxic. So, you can use other forms of support that are available. You have the ability to make your own support system whether it be friends, counselors, church, gym class, a club for your hobby, support groups, and so much more.

A positive support can mean numerous things to different people, but the foundation of the relationship should be positive. It should encourage you to be open, honest, and comfortable. This does not mean that the person has to always agree with you, but when they have advice and critiques it should come out of love. If you discern that this person may not be trustworthy pray before sharing. You deserve nothing less than positive people in your corner. As the scripture says when you have two or three people gathered who are praying for you, encouraging you, and wanting the best for you, God is there. Having a support system has so many benefits. It will help you grow as an individual because it will challenge your viewpoint. It allows you to see things from another perspective. It is easy to feel like God is not there when you are in a hard situation. But if you shift your perspective, you will see that God never left you. The power of unity is beautiful to God, this is why He tells us to love our neighbor as we do ourselves. Imagine trying to push a car by yourself, you may be able to move it some, but now you're exhausted and tired and ready to give up. Now imagine 1 or 2 other people helping you along. Everyone has the same goal which is getting the car into a safe place and on one accord.

Now moving the car became less challenging. You gain more power in reaching your goal when you have positive support versus doing it by yourself.

Challenge

Make a list of the things you value in a friend or a support. Then make a list of people that you would consider a positive support.

Prayer

Heavenly Father, reveal to me what positive support I have in my corner right now. Open my eyes and increase my discernment, so I can choose to be vulnerable with people that will help me out of love. I want to build kingdom connections, so I can grow as an individual and closer to you. In Jesus name, Amen.

Day 26

No Such Thing As Wasted Time

"For everything there is a season, and a time for every matter under heaven: a time to be born, and a time to die; a time to plant, and a time to pluck up what is planted; a time to kill, and a time to heal; a time to break down. And a time to build up; a time to weep, and a time to laugh; a time to mourn, and a time to dance; a time to cast away stones, and a time to gather stones together; a time to embrace, and a time to refrain from embracing." – Ecclesiastes 3:1-22

There is a time for everything. There will be times that you feel like you can conquer the world; and there will also be times when you feel depressed and like nothing is going right. These ups and downs let you know that you are living! In life we go through different seasons. You will experience spring when the things that you harvested finally bloom, fall when things began to break off, winter when you store up what is needed and summer when you bask in the sun and enjoy. These seasons are intentional. Nothing you are going through or have gone through is a waste. It is so easy to feel like you have wasted your time. I personally struggled with this in the past when I finally let go of a toxic five-and-a-half year relationship. I could not help but think "wow, how could I be so naïve" and "I wasted so much time on a relationship that did not even work." At the end of the day, it was something I went through, and it is too late to change the past. I could have been bitter about the amount of time that was "wasted," but instead I took time to stop and reflect on how I could grow from it. It took me a year to get back on my feet and truly heal from those wounds. Sometimes I notice that I am still healing. Nevertheless, I was grateful because in that year I a better understanding of myself and a deeper relationship with God. Plus, I was no longer connected to that toxic relationship that had caused me so much pain. The point I am trying to make is, it is so easy to feel like we have wasted our time journeying through situations that seem to only have dead ends. Our perspective makes a difference. If God allowed you to go through it, He will see you through it. God has already mapped out the path He desires for us to take. He did not create us to be robots. He knew that sometimes we would choose our own way instead of His, but He is gracious. Sometimes God will let us go our own way because there is a lesson that needs to be learned from that place. God has made room for our errors, and He still finds a way to get glory out of our situation. This does not just apply to relationships (romantic or casual). It also applies to anything you felt like you wasted your time on. You have to understand that God does not operate in time because He is eternal. Nonetheless, when you feel like your time was "wasted" take a moment to pause and see what the lesson was. This is a crucial step that will prevent you from falling into the same situation again. Time does not matter because our God is a restorer and when He feels like the time is right He will restore everything that was taken away from you, but you have to learn the lesson first and choose to let go.

Challenge

Create two columns on a sheet of paper. On the left, make a list of things you considered a waste of time. On the right, make a list beside it identifying things you would like God to restore the "wasted time" with.

Prayer

Lord God, I know that you are in control of everything. I thank you for your protection as I continue to journey through life. Help me to see things from more of a spiritual sense, leaning more on your understanding than my own. Continue to renew my mind and clear my vision so I can view things from a healthy perspective. Lord help me to learn the lessons that need to be learned so I can embark on the next chapter in life that you have for me. In Jesus name, Amen.

Day 27

Finding Your Voice

"The tongue has the power of life and death."
– Proverbs 18:21

The devil tried to convince me that my voice was useless. After being in toxic and abusive situations, I was conditioned to not speak on how I felt because in those relationships it felt pointless. I went from being strong and vocal, to weak and powerless in a matter of months. I began shrinking to make others feel comfortable. This trickled into other areas of my life. It took time to find my voice again and to feel like it carried value.

As you go through traumatic experiences, it can be easy to lose your identify and voice. What I have learned in my healing journey is that choosing to be silent was actually keeping me in bondage. I was beginning to have mental break downs due to all the unforgiveness and hurt I was silently carrying. I did not start my healing journey until I began being honest with myself. I found myself asking God to help me with the pain. I slowly began vocalizing the traumatic experiences I had gone through with people I trusted. I never would have guessed how many other women had similar stories and how my testimony would empower them to overcome their trauma. As I continued to find my voice, I noticed that my story began to change. I went from being a victim to a victor because God shifted my mindset.

How you feel and your thoughts matter. If something is making you feel "some kind of way," then give voice to that matter. If you don't, you will continue to find yourself in the same predicaments over and over again. I found myself in the same types of relationships until I finally learned to speak up for myself and set healthy boundaries. In the beginning it may not feel comfortable, but I promise the more you do it, the more you will learn your voice and your flow.

The Bible says there is power in the tongue. You can use your words to build yourself up or cut yourself down. Be mindful of the things you say to yourself. Always speak life over yourself. You can also use your words to end things that are not good for you. This does not mean you have to be rude, but you teach people how to treat you and communication is an effective way to do that. Sometimes the other person doesn't know that something is an issue until you address it. In order to have a healthy relationship, whether romantic, casual, professional, or with God, you must effectively communicate. The Bible tells us that if we have a perceived offense with someone, we should let them know. This is because there is power in releasing how you feel and not holding it in. There is also power and freedom in being able to communicate how you feel. Of course, be wise and pick your battles, but do not let trauma from your past hold you back from finding your voice. There is someone out there that needs to hear your story in a way that only you can tell it. You got this!

Challenge

Identify areas you may have been timid to speak in and areas you may over speak in. Pay attention to people, places, situations and emotions. Identify any patterns you noticed with the list you created. Doing this will help you to be mindful of areas you may need to grow as you find your voice.

Prayer

Lord the enemy tried to steal my voice, but I thank you for protecting me. Give me the confidence I need to be able to speak my truth so that I can heal. I rebuke any attacks that are after my voice. I renounce the lies that the enemy has told me about my voice being useless. I renounce the negative things that I have spoken over myself. I renounce the lies of the enemy that I chose to believe. I break the chains of bondage right now. God guide my tongue so that I speak life into myself and others. In Jesus name, Amen.

Day 28

Setting Boundaries

"Above all else, guard your heart, for everything you do flows from it." — Proverbs 4:23

Proverbs 4:23 tells us the importance of guarding our heart. It is important because everything we do flows from our heart. If we have a broken heart, there is a high likelihood that we will respond from a broken place instead of a healed place. When people think of guarding their heart, especially after being hurt, they often think that putting up walls will protect them. Walls will definitely keep out negative things, but the unfortunate part is, they also keep out the positive. With a wall, you are refusing to let hurt in, but love can't get in either. Walls also put a strain on our relationship with God. How are we supposed to do God's work with a wall up? Your wall is now limiting Him. Believe it or not you hurt yourself more when you put walls up.

When God says guard your heart, He is referring to setting healthy boundaries. Throughout the Bible, God sets boundaries for all of us. His commandments are an example of boundaries. These boundaries are designed to aid us in getting closer to Him and also to protect us from heartbreak and evil. Boundaries are more like gates. With gates you have the control. You choose the positive things you want to let in and you also choose what negative things you want to keep in or escort out. In order to make wise choices regarding what you should or should not let in, your heart has to be whole. This means you have to forgive and let go because following a broken heart will deceive you.

In order to set healthy boundaries, you have to be assertive. You have to know what you stand for, your morals, and your values. Saying "no" can sometimes be challenging, but the more you do it the easier it will become. If it goes against what is best for you, then you have to put yourself first, and that's okay. This is how you maintain your peace and healing. Sometimes compromise is okay, but it depends on the situation. It can be hard trying to figure out what is best for you, but the good thing is we serve a God that will help you identify what's best. You just have to pay attention to the red flags or signs mentioned in the previous challenge. Break down those walls that isolate you and start building gates!

Challenge

Identify areas in your life that you may need to set boundaries in, and then be intentional about setting healthy boundaries.

Prayer

Heavenly Father show me the walls I created that kept me away from you and doing your will. Lord, help me to break these walls down because I no longer want to be stuck. Help me to replace these walls with gates. Mend my heart so I can learn how to set healthy boundaries that are best for me and according to your will. In Jesus name, Amen.

Day 29

Put On Your Armor

"Therefore put on the full armor of God, so that when the day of evil comes, you may be able to stand your ground, and after you have done everything to stand. Stand firm then, with the belt of truth buckled around your waist, with the breastplate of righteousness in place, and with your feet fitted with the readiness that comes from the gospel of peace. In addition to all this, take up the shield of faith, with which you can extinguish all the flaming arrows of the evil one. Take the helmet of salvation and the sword of the Spirit, which is the word of God." – Ephesians 6:13-17

You may have heard the saying, "God hears you, but the devil does too." There was an instance when I cried my heart out praying, and the devil had a counterfeit regurgitating the exact prayer I had prayed that morning when I was alone in front of the entire congregation. It was crazy, but it showed me how real this statement is. I was able to know it was a counterfeit because I had spent time in God's presence and I know His voice. This is why the day one challenge of "Hearing From God" is so important. Oftentimes, you can tell if something is from God or from the enemy based on the heart of the condition. If it is not coming from a place of love and growth, then it is not of God. The battle we are fighting is spiritual. Whether you want to acknowledge that evil principles exist or not is another story, but it does not stop you from being a target. Do you wonder why you keep running into the same people with different faces, or how this person knows how to push your buttons and they just met you? It is a spiritual battle that is not meant for you to fight alone. Ephesians 6: 10-19 talks about what the armor of God is and the importance of wearing it daily. Forgiveness is an area you need to be suited up to protect yourself in at all times. The devil does not sleep. He is ready to attack at any given moment. By praying regularly, reading your Word, and seeking God's face, God will reveal things that can help you better prepare for the situation that is coming or is already present. He adds the super to our natural. Having the armor will also aid you in dealing with offense. Sometimes offenses are forced on us and other times we volunteer to be offended. Ultimately it is your choice how long a matter offends you.

Let's really break down the armor. The Bible first mentions the belt of truth. This is because knowing THE TRUTH is important. We live in a society that encourages us to, "live how you feel," but that is not what God calls us to do. God calls us to live by His truth which is His Word and His purpose for our lives. If you neglect to live in truth, you won't be able to protect yourself from the enemy because the Bible tells us that he is the father of lies and deception. This is why I had you renounce the lies of the enemy over your life in a previous challenge. If you don't do this, he will continue to hold you in bondage because you will be dwelling in his lies.

The next mention is the breastplate of righteousness. Righteousness is not doing all the right things to appear holy, that's self- righteousness. God's righteousness was given to use when we take the steps to become saved. This righteousness cleanses us of the shame and guilt we picked up from the past and the lies that the devil tries to drill in our heads. The righteousness that God gives allows us to be right with Him and free to be who He has called us to be regardless of where we come from or what we have done. It takes away the burden of having to be perfect in order to have a relationship, when really God chose us in our imperfection and still felt like we were good enough.

This brings us to the armor for your feet, which are fitted with the gospel of peace. Your mind is a powerful thing and the thoughts and beliefs you entertain can affect you and the outcome of the battle. Trials and tribulations will come, but the gospel of peace allows you to be confident that the battle is won and that you will come out victorious regardless of how things seem. It allows you to stand up right in truth and God's promises. It also gives you the ability to move where God is telling you to go with peace and stability because you are confident that God will follow through. Whatever the enemy throws at you will not move you because you are firm in God's peace. The only way you will lose this peace is if you give it away.

After this you grab your shield of faith. The devil's goal is to attack your mind because if he can attack your mind then it affects your emotions, which will affect your behavior. Here's a prime example. If Satan can provoke a thought that makes you feel like you are "worthless," then you can fall into depression, which now affects your ability to connect with other people. This is why the shield is so important. It is a representation of the faith that we have that God will cover and protect us. The shield will cover and protect you from anything the devil tries to throw at you physically, mentally, and emotionally because our faith is in God, not the lies of the enemy.

This brings me to the next piece of armor, the helmet of salvation. The helmet of salvation is knowledge that we gain from God's Word that lets us know that as believers we have been rescued from our own demise and depravity as long as we keep our minds on Him. You must be intentional about feeding your mind principles, scriptures, and teachings from the Word so that you can be ready when the enemy tries to attack.

The last piece of armor is the sword of the Spirit. Notice that it is the only piece of armor you can use to defend yourself. This is why it is so important to feed your mind and spirit with the Word because when it's time to swing your sword, it is really God's Word that you are using to fight your battles. When you are going through a hardship, you can call His Word forth and use it against the enemy. God's Word cuts the devil down and puts him back in his place, but it is hard to use the sword when you have not spent time in God's presence or read His Word. The best way to defeat the enemy with minimal scars is by spending time with God, getting into your Word, and being obedient, so suit up and protect your freedom, peace, and joy!

Challenge

Pray and ask God to help you suit up in the armor, so that you can protect yourself from dangers seen and unseen. Also, learn more about the armor so you can properly suit up.

Prayer

Lord God help me to suit up for this battle. Open my eyes so that I can see the signs and open my ears so that I can hear your direction and instruction during this time. Continue to protect me from danger seen and unseen. And increase my appetite for your word because it is the only truth. Thank you for keeping me in Jesus name, Amen.

Day 30

Purposing Your Pain

"For I know the plans I have for you," declares the LORD, "plans to prosper you and not to harm you, plans to give you hope and a future."
— Jeremiah 29:11

I am so proud of you for making it through this challenge. You are so resilient. Your past is supposed to be a lesson, not a jail sentence. Understand that the decisions you made in your past, and the situations you have been working on throughout your healing journey, were not meant to enslave you, but to help you grow. Everything we endure is for a reason. We have to endure some storms in order to really appreciate the beauty of a rainbow. In order to have victory, you had to overcome something. I hope that throughout the course of this book, you have come to the revelation that what you went through has the ability to elevate you to the next level. The beautiful thing about God is He does not need perfect pieces to make a masterpiece, He just needs your obedience. When He created you, He knew that you were good because you were made by a God who makes no mistakes. When those tragic events happened, understand that God was with you. When the devil tried to take you out and tear you down, God said I can use that to take you further and lift you higher.

You have to understand the importance your mindset plays in the matter because your circumstances and the people around you aren't going to hold you back, but your thoughts will. My prayer and desire are for you to learn to trust God when things are going "bad." We often say everything happens for a reason, but that also includes the things that may not have gone the way we desired. When God makes promises, it is normally to give us hope in the midst of a storm. People often use the scripture, "For I know the plans I have for you," but do not understand the context behind it. This passage was written from Jeremiah to the people of Jerusalem that had been exiled to Babylon. To be exiled means to be banned from your home or nation. These people were in an unfamiliar place and they were suffering. They wanted to be rescued immediately, but God informed them, "I know this may not feel good right now, but if you just hold on to my promises you will make it out of here and back to your home." In the midst of hardship we often feel like we are the furthest from God. We want to be rescued immediately, but in those moments when things seem the hardest, we are actually the closest.

Jeremiah 29:12-14, *"Then you will call on me and come and pray to me, and I will listen to you. You will seek me and find me when you seek me with all your heart. I will be found by you."*

Did you catch that? Although the Jews felt like they were broken, in bondage, defeated, and hurting, God did not leave them and encouraged His people to call on Him. Just because you feel like you are suffering, in bondage, worthless, defeated, and however else you may feel, God is encouraging you to take the time to find Him in the midst of what seems like darkness. There is always light in the midst of darkness, but you have to be mindful of your positioning. If you turn your back on the light, it will seem dark. Nothing you endure is worthless or in vain. It all has purpose. We do ourselves a disservice when we choose not to find purpose in our pain. It will all work out for your benefit as long as you continue to be faithful and obedient. Understand that when the devil tried to destroy you, God used that very situation to build your capacity for your next step. The devil cannot stop God's plans for you. Stop reliving the hurt, shame, and mistakes of the past. It's time to move forward. God has you right where He wants you. He's made provisions for your errors. As this book ends, your journey continues. Remember the things God has promised you whether from scriptures that uplift you or things that He told you in your private time with Him. Those promises were given to you so that you could be encouraged and know that God is fighting for you even when you don't feel it. There is a difference between knowing and feeling. Feelings are temporary, but God's promises are facts. I challenge you to put His promises all around your room, in your car, as your screen saver, or even on your mirror, so you can be reminded that He is with you. Healing is an intentional daily battle. Some days may be better than others, but if you are obedient and hold on to God's promises you will overcome. Even when you feel like you cannot go on, He is always close to the broken. Trust the process and watch your life transform.

Challenge

Make a list of the promises God has made you and continue to hold on to them as you go through your healing journey. This will keep you motivated during the tough times. You got this!

Prayer

Thank you Lord for watching over me and bringing me to this very moment. Open my eyes so that I can see the beauty in where I currently am. Reveal how I can begin giving purpose to my pain. Renew my mind so that I can begin to transform my thoughts, reality, and life. I pray that you would continue to navigate me through this healing journey and allow me to use the tactics I have learned in the book to refrain from self-inflicted pain. In the mighty name of Jesus, Amen.

www.ingramcontent.com/pod-product-compliance
Lightning Source LLC
Chambersburg PA
CBHW060847050426
42453CB00008B/875